TABLE OF CONTENTS

Chapter 1

Introduction and Aim of the Project

WannaCry Ransomware attack was a cyberattack on May 12, 2017, by the WannaCry ransomware crypto-worm, attacking computers based on the Microsoft Windows System by encrypting the computer's data and asked for ransoms through one of the most popular and widely used cryptocurrencies, Bitcoin. It asked for 300$ worth of Bitcoins to decrypt the computer's data. More than, 200,000 computers in over 150 countries were under the attack. Some of the victims of this widespread ransomware were Honda, Nissan, FedEx, and the UK's National Health Service(NHS).

Within few hours of the attack, WannaCry was neutralized temporarily by a security analyst who discovered a "kill switch" facilitating malware termination. Instead of this neutralization, many affected computers remained encrypted and could not be used unless the victims paid the amount or could reverse the encryption. Despite all efforts to contain its impact, the underlying dynamics of such ransomware are still a challenge to comprehend. WannaCry's behavior, especially its spreading mechanisms, encryption methods, and communication with affected systems, is not completely understood.

This lack of profound knowledge makes it difficult to design effective countermeasures, detect new variants, and prevent similar attacks. Static behavior is inspected in majority of analyses, leaving a gap for dynamic analysis, which is needed to examine how the malware acts when executed in real-time, such as its network traffic, behavior on the system files, and propagation via networks.

Thus, the problem is the absence of adequate knowledge of how WannaCry operates dynamically, especially in a controlled environment, and how it leverages system weaknesses to spread and encrypt data. Without this kind of knowledge, it is hard to develop efficient mitigation, detection, and prevention measures for such ransomware attacks. This project aims to bridge this gap by performing a comprehensive dynamic analysis of WannaCry, thereby providing actionable knowledge for enhancing cybersecurity defense against similar attacks.

WannaCry spread by using a loophole in the Windows OS named "EternalBlue". The US National Security Agency(NSA) had developed this exploit for its use, but it was stolen and released to the public by a group known as the Shadow Brokers after the NSA was itself compromised. EternalBlue only worked on older, unpatched versions of Microsoft Windows, but enough environments were running such versions of the Windows operating system that enabled WannaCry's prompt spread.

As we know, the worm is a software program that is considered malicious as it automatically spread itself to several computers connected in the network. A worm uses susceptibility of the operating system to jump from one computer to another. WannaCry was unique and one of a kind because it combined ransomware with a worm, exploiting the NSA's description of EternalBlue.

The importance of analyzing ransomware is that, till now, there have been studies that mainly focused on Static analysis by using tools available for reverse engineering, such as Ghidra, Cutter, Radare2, Binary Ninja, etc. Using these tools, we can conveniently analyze the codes generated by each of the following and then look for malicious content inside this code.

But, by doing a Dynamic analysis of ransomware in a virtual environment, we can study the changes and effects on the Windows OS in real time. We can do so by installing VirtualBox or Windows Sandbox for virtual environment setup, then installing a window, taking a snapshot of the current state of the window, that is, before installing the Wannacry.exe on Windows, so that after dynamic analysis, we can restore the current state of the window.

The project aims to perform a thorough dynamic analysis of the WannaCry ransomware in an attempt to identify its behavior, propagation vectors, encryption methods, and how it affects compromised systems. The analysis entails running the ransomware in a virtual environment to track its interaction with the operating system, network, and other program components.

Important objectives are:

1. Review WannaCry Payload: See how the ransomware infects machines, the way it installs, and the processes it follows upon execution.
2. Learn about Communication Patterns: Review the pattern of how WannaCry speaks to its Command and Control (C&C) servers and methods it utilizes to receive the encryption keys, as well as other orders.
3. Review Encryption Mechanism: Determine the method WannaCry encrypts its content, the method it locks down user documents, and the decryption methodology.
4. Monitor Propagation Tactics: Analyze how WannaCry propagates within local networks and how it uses vulnerabilities like the SMB vulnerability (EternalBlue).
5. Impact Analysis: Quantify the effect on system resources, network traffic, and overall functionality during and post-infection.
6. Create Mitigation Tactics: Based on the analysis, suggest and test defense mechanisms to reduce the threat of WannaCry and other ransomware attacks in the future.

The result of this dynamic analysis paves a way for better understanding of ransomware behavior, offering insights for enhancing detection, prevention, and response techniques.

Chapter 2

Background Study and Research Gap

WannaCry ransomware is one of the most famous and widespread recent cyberattacks. It appeared in May 2017 and instantly attacked hundreds of thousands of computers across over 150 nations, predominantly companies, medical facilities, and government bodies. The assault primarily leveraged a Microsoft Windows Server Message Block (SMB) protocol weakness known as EternalBlue, primarily discovered by the National Security Agency (NSA) and later distributed by the hacking collective Shadow Brokers. This exposed flaw allowed WannaCry to propagate between computers over networks and to encrypt computer files on an affected machine before requesting payment in Bitcoin in exchange for an unlock key.

What made WannaCry most dangerous was that it had worm-like behavior. When a single computer in a network was corrupted, WannaCry propagated to the rest of the computers without any action by the user, thereby becoming highly contagious and capable of inflicting huge damage within a short period.

The encryption used by WannaCry was based on the RSA and AES encryption methodologies, which locked users out of their files and demanded payment of a ransom to obtain a decryption key. Besides encryption, WannaCry utilized **Command and Control (C&C) servers** for remote communication, allowing it to spread its attack and distribute ransomware payloads to new machines.

Some other strategies proposed are as follows :

In [1], In this paper, researchers analyzed the advent of malware creation tools in recent years has eased the development of new versions of pre-existing malware samples. Generally, Anti-Virus company styles new malware samples manually to figure their maliciousness and produce their signatures. This paper offers a novel way to automatically cluster malware variants into malware families on the basis of structured control flow graphs of these malware instances.

In [2], In this paper, researchers study procedures to determine and dissect malicious software that are imperative to improve security systems. The adaptability of Software-Defined Networking (SDN) gives a shot to develop a malware analysis architecture integrating different systems and network profile configurations. In this paper, we design an architecture specialized in malware analysis using SDN to dynamically reconfigure the network environment based on malware actions.

In [3], In this paper researchers define a guide to intelligence for cyber threat: Using the wisdom about opponent to win the war against such attacks.

In [4], In this paper, researchers proposed an approach which is anticipated to be useful for automating the method of dissecting a large volume of logs gathered from dynamic malware analysis systems. To automate malware analysis, dynamic malware analysis systems have drawn more attention from both the industry and research communities. Of the various logs gathered by such systems, the API call is a very reliable source of information for distinguishing malware behavior. They propose an unsupervised way to extract API call topics from a large corpus of API calls. Through analysis of the API call logs gathered from thousands of malware instances, we proved that the extracted API call topics can hunt similar malware samples.

In [5], In this paper, researchers proposed an approach for recognizing malware and characterizing it into either known or novel, i.e., previously unseen malware families. Malware, i.e., malicious software, defines one of the main cybersecurity hazards today. Over the last decade, malware has been unfolding in terms of their complexity and the variation of attack vectors. The proposed approach relies on a Random Forests classifier for performing both malware detection and family characterization.

In [6], In this paper, researchers present the Malware Forensics Field Guide for Linux Systems as an easily available reference which shows students the necessary tools required to do computer forensics analysis at the crime scene. It is especially for Linux-based systems, where new malware is created every day. The authors are world-renowned personalities in inspecting and dissecting malicious code.

In [7], In this paper, researchers gave away a dynamic analysis system named UNVEIL that is especially designed to find out ransomware. The key understanding of the analysis is that to make attack successful, ransomware must intervene with the user's files or desktop. UNVEIL automatically creates a virtual user environment and traces when ransomware collaborates with user data. In parallel, the approach detects changes to the system's desktop which shows ransomware-like behavior. UNVEIL can point out previously unrecognized evasive ransomware that was hidden from the antimalware industry.

In [8], In this paper, researchers studied that Ransomware attacks have emerged as a significant cybersecurity threat, impacting organizations globally, including the South African public sector. This research conducted a narrative review aimed at investigating the South African public sector's capability to address ransomware attacks. The review examined news articles, reports, and literature from databases such as Scopus, Google Scholar, and ScienceDirect. Furthermore, this review explored the evolving landscape of ransomware, including its modus operandi and impacts. The findings revealed that since 2019, ten different South African public sector entities have been targeted by ransomware, with one entity being hit twice. Based on those findings, this study provided recommendations to strengthen the South African public sector's national defenses and improve its preparedness for future ransomware attacks.

In [9], In this paper, researchers developed a value chain and depictions of the actors involved in this economy from their data. Ransomware is an epidemic that adversely affects the lives of both individuals and large companies, where criminals demand payments to release infected digital assets. In the wake of the ransomware success, Ransomware-as-a-Service (RaaS) has become a franchise offered through darknet marketplaces, allowing ambitious cyber attackers to take part in this disputable economy. Our observations show that RaaS presently seems like a moderate threat, kin to popular opinion. As compared to other types of illegal digital goods, there are preferably few RaaS items offered for sale in darknet marketplaces, often with debatable authenticity.

In [10], In this paper, researchers explain that Crypto-Ransomware exploits techniques of cryptography to take control of personal files and documents and encrypts them. Employing such a technological bound, crypto-ransomware corrupts a variety of platforms and systems. Though several users, no matter individuals or organizations, rehearse insightful security procedures like advanced crypto-ransomware, regular backup can detour these countermeasures, laying down precious data endangered to such extortion attacks. Due to the irrecoverable nature of its damage, beating crypto-ransomware becomes difficult. Though various studies have been acquitted to handle the crypto-ransomware detection problem, most of them handles it from a malware perspective.

Chapter 3

Tools/Platform, Hardware and Software Requirement Specification

(DFD, ER/UML)

TOOLS and PLATFORM :

In order to effectively perform a dynamic analysis of WannaCry ransomware, a number of tools and platforms are required for controlled execution, monitoring, analysis, and reporting. These tools will assist in the understanding of WannaCry's behavior, propagation, and encryption methods. Moreover, analysis will need to be done in a secure, isolated environment in order to avoid any accidental spreading of the ransomware to key systems.

Hardware Specifications

Host Workstation/Computer:

- Processor: Minimum dual-core processor, preferably multi-core processor for better performance.
- RAM: A minimum of 4 GB of RAM (8 GB advisable) to accommodate multiple virtual machines and analysis programs to be used in tandem.
- Disk Storage: 100 GB HDD or SSD (to keep the operating system images, malware data for analysis, and logs).
- Graphics: Built-in or dedicated graphics card should be enough

for routine operation, but not essential for this kind of analysis.

- Network: A solid network connection (for outside communication, tool downloads, and inspection of network traffic).

Virtualization Hardware (for establishing isolated environments):

- Host Machine: Physical computer able to run virtualization software such as VMware or VirtualBox.

Software Requirements

Operating Systems:

- Windows Operating System (for infected machine simulation): The malware is designed to attack Windows-based systems (Windows 7, 8, 10, or older versions susceptible to EternalBlue). Various versions of Windows (ideally in virtual environments) must be utilized to test the effect of the malware.

- Linux OS: There is a requirement for a Linux-based platform (e.g., Kali Linux) for operating network monitoring software and helping with the analysis of network traffic, malware activity, and reverse engineering.

Virtualization Platform:

- VMware Workstation/VMware ESXi: A powerful platform for virtual environment creation and management. It provides isolation of the WannaCry ransomware from any production network and ensures security.

- Oracle VM VirtualBox: A VMware alternative, this free virtualization software can be employed to build several virtual machines for analysis.

Reverse-Engineering tools:

- Ghidra: Debuggers and Disassemblers to reverse engineer the WannaCry ransomware binary code, helps understand how it works and the changes it does to the system it infects.

- Cutter: Cutter is a an open-source reverse engineering platform powered by Rizin, and is available for free. It is designed to be progressive and an accommodated reverse engineering platform, keeping the user experience in mind. Cutter was developed by reverse engineers for reverse engineers. This tool decompiles the object code into High-Level Language code (like C).

- Radare2: A libre/free tool for smoothing multiple low-level tasks like reverse engineering, forensics, debugging, binary analysis, exploiting, etc. It is made up of many libraries which are expanded with programs and plugins that can be made to operate on its own with almost any programming language. This tool converts the binary code into assembly instructions.

- Ret-Dec: It is a retargetable machine-code decompiler developed by Avast which is rooted on LLVM. This decompiler is not restricted to any specific target architecture, executable file format or operating system. It can be used for static analysis of executable files with detailed information. It can turn binaries (.exe files) into readable C code, which is helpful for our malware analysis. This tool converts the machine code into High-Level Language code (like C or a similar HLL language).

- Binary Ninja: Binary Ninja is a disassembler, interactive decompiler, integrated debugger, and a platform for binary analysis that serves as a reverse engineering platform developed by Vector 35 Inc. Using this, we can disassemble and visualize a binary file in both graph-based and linear views. The Debugger is written in C++ and is shipped with BN as a plugin. It is the most advanced platform for binary analysis and has a stack of unique related intermediate languages. High-Level IL is the default view, we can see it and observe that it almost reads like pseudocode. This tool decompiles the object code into High-Level Language code (like C or C++) and also disassembles the code in to assembly instructions.

- Obj Dump: Obj-dump is a lightweight and powerful tool for inspecting and disassembling binaries which forms a perfect basis for basic static analysis, and it is built with Kali Linux. It comes installed as a part of the package named "binutils". This tool can be used as a disassembler, to view your executable file in assembly language.

DFD & ER Diagram

Data Flow Diagram(DFD)

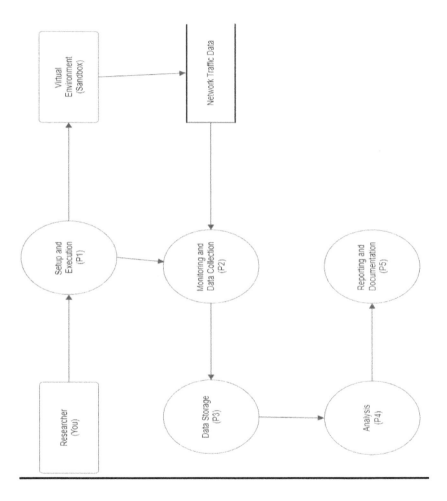

ER Diagram

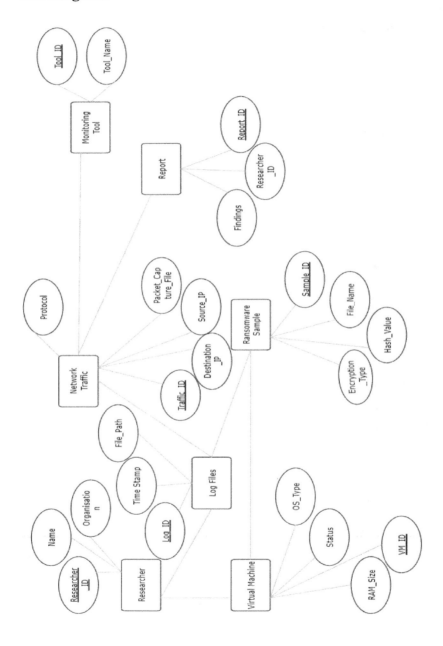

Chapter 4

Proposed work and Methodology

4.1 Static Analysis

In this part, first we install Wannacry.exe (by default, in your Downloads folder) and then analyze it with the help of various reverse engineering tools, which are as follows:

Let's see how to use and install them, and analyze the .exe file.

4.1.1 Ghidra

Ghidra is a software for reverse engineering (SRE) framework created by the NSA's Research Directorate. It consists of a suite of fully-featured, exclusive software analysis tools enabling users to dissect compiled code on several platforms, including macOS, Windows, and Linux. It can be used for assembly, decompilation, disassembly, debugging, graphing, emulation, and scripting. It can be run in both automated and user-interactive modes.

Ghidra SRE credentials are applicable to a diverse set of problems concerned with dissecting malicious code and identifying deep insights for NSA analysts who seek a better comprehension of potential sensitivity in networks as well as systems.

This tool decompiles the object code into High-Level Language code (like C).

Steps to be followed to install and use Ghidra:

- Releases · NationalSecurityAgency/ghidra Download the latest version for Linux.
- The zip folder is downloaded by default in your Downloads folder.
- Open Downloads, and extract the zip folder.
- Open Terminal
- Navigate to Downloads, using the command in Fig. 4.1.1.1

Figure 4.1.1.1 This is a terminal window in Kali Linux. The kali written in blue indicates the username as well as the hostname with a special character(~) informing us about the current directory in which we are operating. In the above figure, the command run is "cd Downloads," which takes us to the Downloads Directory, which is usually present inside the home directory.

- Navigate to Ghidra, using the command in Fig. 4.1.1.2

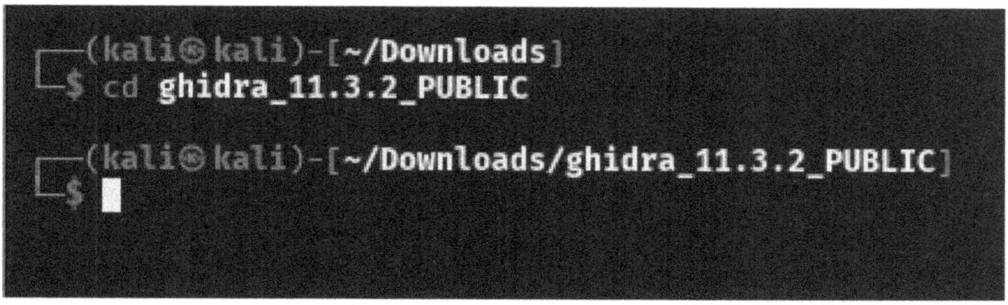

Figure 4.1.1.2. This image tells us that we are using the Kali Linux terminal, and we are inside our Downloads Directory, which contains a folder ghidra_11.3.2_PUBLIC. We want to change the current directory to the directory present inside the Downloads folder to access Ghidra resources.

- Check for Java version, using the command in Fig. 4.1.1.3

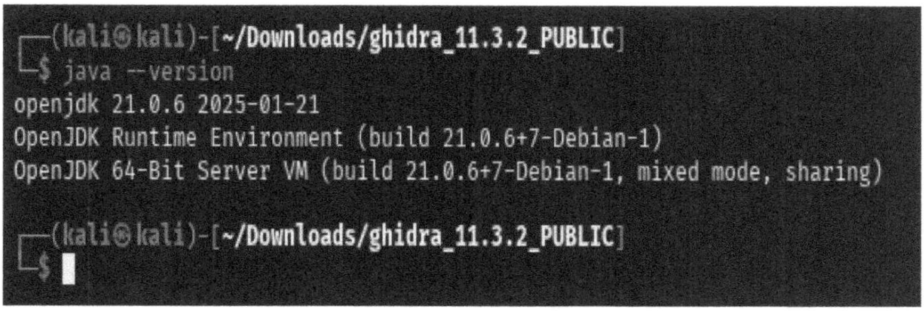

Figure 4.1.1.3 This image tells us that we are using the Kali Linux terminal, and we are inside our ghidra_11.3.2_PUBLIC Directory which is present inside Downloads and we have run a command "java –version" to check whether Java is installed on our system or not, and if present then what version of JDK is there.

If it displays something like this, then Java is installed in your environment; else, download JDK latest version.

- Now, ghidra is ready to be used for analysis.

4.1.2   Cutter

Cutter is a an open-source reverse engineering platform powered by Rizin, and is available for free. It is designed to be progressive and an accommodated reverse engineering platform, keeping the user experience in mind. Cutter was developed by reverse engineers for reverse engineers.

This tool decompiles the object code into High-Level Language code (like C).

Steps to be followed to install and use Cutter:

- https://cutter.re/ Download Cutter.
- The Cutter app image is downloaded by default in your Downloads folder.
- Open Terminal
- Navigate to Downloads, using the command in Fig. 4.1.2.1

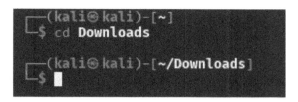

Figure 4.1.2.1 This is a terminal window in Kali Linux. The kali written in blue indicates the username as well as the hostname with a special character(~) informing us about the current directory in which we are operating. In the above figure, the command run is "cd Downloads," which takes us to the Downloads Directory, which is usually present inside the home directory.

- Make your cutter tool executable and run, using the command in Fig. 4.1.2.2

```
┌──(kali㉿kali)-[~/Downloads]
└─$ chmod +x Cutter-v2.3.4-Linux-x86_64.AppImage
```

Figure 4.1.2.2 This is a terminal window of Kali Linux, which tells that we are inside the Downloads folder and there is an app image of the Cutter tool inside the Downloads folder, and through this command "chmod +x Cutter-v2.3.4-Linux-x86_64.AppImage" we are making it executable or giving permission to execute.

- Now, cutter is ready to be used for analysis.

4.1.3 Radare2

A libre/free tool for smoothing multiple low-level tasks like reverse engineering, forensics, debugging, binary analysis, exploiting, etc. It is made up of many libraries which are expanded with programs and plugins that can be made to operate on it's own with almost any programming language.

This tool converts the binary code into assembly instructions.

Steps to be followed to install and use radare2:

- Open Terminal
- Install Kali, using the command in Fig. 4.1.3.1

Figure 4.1.3.1 This is a terminal window in the Kali Linux. The kali written in blue indicates the username as well as the hostname with a special character(~) informing us about the current directory in which we are operating. In the above Fig. the command run is "sudo apt install radare2" for installing radare2 on our Linux OS and asks for password to proceed with installation.

- Now, radare2 is ready to be used for analysis.

4.1.4 Ret-Dec

It is a retargetable machine-code decompiler developed by Avast which is rooted on LLVM. This decompiler is not restricted to any specific target architecture, executable file format or operating system. It can be used for static analysis of executable files with detailed information. It can turn binaries (.exe files) into readable C code, which is helpful for our malware analysis.

This tool converts the machine code into High-Level Language code (like C or a similar HLL language).

<u>Steps to be followed to install and use ret-dec:</u>

- https://sourceforge.net/projects/redtdec.mirror/   Download   it from here.
- By default, it is downloaded into your Downloads folder.
- Unzip it then open terminal
- Navigate to ret-dec, using the command in Fig. 4.1.4.1

Figure 4.1.4.1 This is a terminal window in the Kali Linux. The kali written in blue indicates the username as well as the hostname with a special character(~) informing us about the current directory in which we are operating. In the above Fig. the command run is "cd Downloads" which takes us to the Downloads Directory, which is usually present inside the home directory. Then, we navigate inside ret-dec folder which is inside Downloads.

- Run the command in Fig. 4.1.4.2

```
┌──(kali㉿kali)-[~/Downloads/retdec]
└─$ mkdir build && cd build
```

Figure 4.1.4.2 This is a terminal window in the Kali Linux. The kali written in blue indicates the username as well as the hostname with a special character(~) informing us about the current directory in which we are operating, in the above figure we are inside the ret-dec folder and the command "mkdir" creates a new directory named build in the current directory.

- Now, run the command in Fig. 4.1.4.3

```
┌──(kali㉿kali)-[~/Downloads/retdec]
└─$ cd build

┌──(kali㉿kali)-[~/Downloads/retdec/build]
└─$ cmake ..
-- Found OpenSSL: /usr/lib/x86_64-linux-gnu/libcrypto.so
```

Figure 4.1.4.3 This is a terminal window in the Kali Linux. The kali written in blue indicates the username as well as the hostname with a special character(~) informing us about the current directory in which we are operating, in the above figure we were inside the ret-dec then we navigate to build inside ret-dec and then we run "cmake .." to initialize the build configuration using CMake, which points to the parent directory where cmakelists.txt is located.

- Now, build it (takes some time), using the command in Fig. 4.1.4.4

```
┌──(kali㉿kali)-[~/Downloads/retdec/build]
└─$ make -j$(nproc)
[   1%] Built target authenticode
[   1%] Built target stb
```

Figure 4.1.4.4 This is a terminal window in the Kali Linux. The kali written in blue indicates the username as well as the hostname with a special character(~) informing us about the current directory in which we are operating, in the above figure we are inside build folder and we run the command "make -j$nproc" after the configuration is complete, so that it starts compiling RetDec using all CPU cores. This process takes some time depending on your system's power.

- Now, ret-dec is ready to be used for analysis.

4.1.5   Binary Ninja

Binary Ninja is a disassembler, interactive decompiler, integrated debugger, and a platform for binary analysis that serves as a reverse engineering platform developed by Vector 35 Inc. Using this, we can disassemble and visualize a binary file in both graph-based and linear views. The Debugger is written in C++ and is shipped with BN as a plugin. It is the most advanced platform for binary analysis and has a stack of unique related intermediate languages. High-Level IL is the default view, we can see it and observe that it almost reads like pseudocode.

This tool decompiles the object code into High-Level Language code (like C or C++) and also disassembles the code in to assembly instructions.

<u>Steps to be followed to install and use Binary Ninja:</u>

- https://binary.ninja/free/ Select Download for Linux
- The zip folder is downloaded by default in your Downloads folder.
- Unzip it and then open the terminal
- Navigate to the Binary Ninja directory, using the command in Fig. 4.1.5.1

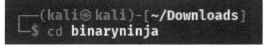

Figure 4.1.5.1 This is a terminal window in the Kali Linux. The kali written in blue indicates the username as well as the hostname with a special character(~) informing us about the current directory in which we are operating. In the above Fig., we are inside the Downloads Directory, and we want to navigate inside binary ninja using the command "cd binaryninja".

- Make it executable, using the command in Fig. 4.1.5.2

```
┌──(kali㉿kali)-[~/Downloads/binaryninja]
└─$ chmod +x binaryninja
```

Figure 4.1.5.2 This is a terminal window of the Kali Linux which tells that we are inside the binaryninja folder and this command "chmod +x binaryninja" is run because we are making it executable or giving permission to execute for the analysis of Wannacry.exe to find patterns and irrelevant function calls.

- Now, binary ninja is ready to be used for analysis.

4.1.6   Obj-dump

Obj-dump is a lightweight and powerful tool for inspecting and disassembling binaries which forms a perfect basis for basic static analysis, and it is built with Kali Linux. It comes installed as a part of the package named "binutils".

This tool can be used as a disassembler, to view your executable file in assembly language.

Steps to follow to use obj-dump:

- Check whether obj-dump is installed or not, using the command in Fig. 4.1.6.1

```
┌──(kali㉿kali)-[~/Downloads]
└─$ objdump --version
GNU objdump (GNU Binutils for Debian) 2.44
Copyright (C) 2025 Free Software Foundation, Inc.
This program is free software; you may redistribute it under the terms of
the GNU General Public License version 3 or (at your option) any later version.
This program has absolutely no warranty.
```

Figure 4.1.6.1 This is a terminal window in the Kali Linux. The kali written in blue indicates the username as well as the hostname with a special character(~) informing us about the current directory in which we are operating. In the above Fig., we are inside Downloads Directory, and we are checking the version of obj-dump which comes as a part of binutils package.

- If it is not installed, then install it using the command "sudo apt install binutils"
- Now, obj-dump is ready to be used for analysis.

4.2 Dynamic Analysis

- In this part, we will setup Windows 10 in Oracle Virtual Box by following the steps mentioned in Chapter 5.
- Then, Windows Defender's real-time protection and ransomware protection needs to be turned off to download Wannacry.exe successfully on our system.
- Now, we run the setup and install Wannacry.exe on our virtual environment and carefully observe the changes it makes to our virtual environment.

Chapter 5

Design/Development

ENVIRONMENTAL SETUP

Setting up VirtualBox or Windows Sandbox

1. Go to google.com
2. Search "VirtualBox" and navigate to "virtualbox.org"
3. Click Download, and then select the platform on which you want to use it (E.g., if you have Windows OS, go for the Windows hosts package)
4. After downloading, run the setup.
5. Follow all the default steps.
6. VirtualBox is installed on your system.

Installing the Windows Operating System

1. Go to google.com
2. Search "Windows 10 download," then navigate to "Download Windows 10 Disc Image (ISO File)"
3. See "Create Windows 10 installation media" and click on Download.
4. Install the Media Creation Tool and follow the steps below

Open > Accept > Create Installation Media > Select Language, Edition, Architecture > Choose Media to use: ISO File > File Name > Save to your PC.

Setting up Windows OS on VirtualBox

1. Open VirtualBox > New in Virtual Box > Name, Select Microsoft Windows as type > Select iso image installed from the media creation tool > Select Windows 10 based on your system type if it is x64-based PC, select 64-bit version > Skip Unattended installation > Next > Base memory(as per your system), Processors (2 CPU) – stay in the green area only > Create a Virtual Hard Disk Now and allocate Disk Size > Next > Finish.

2. After this, go to details, then settings > Network (Bridged Adapter)

3. Start Windows 10 in Virtual Box > Select Lang, Time, Keyboard as per your convenience > Next > Install Now > I don't have a product key > Windows 10 Pro > Accept the license terms then Next > Custom Install > Select Drive then Next > Windows is installing (sit back and relax) > Select region > Select Keyboard > Skip second keyboard layout > Offline account > Limited Experience > Name of user, then

Next > Set password then Next > Set up Security Questions > Not now > Accept > Skip > Not now.

4. You're ready to use Windows in VirtualBox.

Taking a Snapshot of the Windows OS and Installing Ransomware

- Take a snapshot of the windows, so that we can restore the window's current state after installing Wannacry.exe.
- Search for game first iv WannaCry GitHub and go to the repository and download Wannacry.exe
- Then, run Wannacry.exe and carefully observe what changes it made to your operating system.

Installing Kali Linux

Let's install Kali Linux as the operating system to install various tools used for reverse engineering, such as Ghidra, Cutter, Radare2, Ret-Dec, Binary Ninja, and Objdump.

1. Go to google.com
2. Search "Kali Linux Download" and navigate to "kali.org"
3. Go to Virtual Machines, and click on the recommended
4. Download the one with VirtualBox by clicking on the arrow pointing downwards.
5. After downloading, open VirtualBox

6. Click on Tools on the left side, then click Add

7. Navigate to the location where your VM is downloaded and select the ".vbox" file.

8. The default username and password is kali.

Chapter 6

Testing and Implementation

6.1 Static Analysis

Let's see how to use reverse engineering tools installed in 4.1, and analyze the .exe file.

6.1.1 Ghidra

Steps to be followed to use Ghidra:

- Open Terminal
- Navigate to Downloads, using the command in Fig. 6.1.1.1

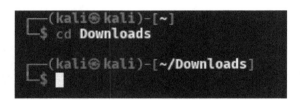

Figure 6.1.1.1 This is a terminal window in Kali Linux. The kali written in blue indicates the username as well as the hostname with a special character(~) informing us about the current directory in which we are operating. In the above figure, the command run is "cd Downloads," which takes us to the Downloads Directory, which is usually present inside the home directory.

- Navigate to Ghidra, using the command in Fig. 6.1.1.2

```
┌──(kali㉿kali)-[~/Downloads]
└─$ cd ghidra_11.3.2_PUBLIC

┌──(kali㉿kali)-[~/Downloads/ghidra_11.3.2_PUBLIC]
└─$ 
```

Figure 6.1.1.2. This image tells us that we are using the Kali Linux terminal, and we are inside our Downloads Directory, which contains a folder ghidra_11.3.2_PUBLIC. We want to change the current directory to the directory present inside the Downloads folder to access Ghidra resources.

- Run Ghidra, using the command in Fig. 6.1.1.3

```
┌──(kali㉿kali)-[~/Downloads/ghidra_11.3.2_PUBLIC]
└─$ ./ghidraRun
```

Figure 6.1.1.3 This image tells us that we are using the Kali Linux terminal, and we are inside our ghidra_11.3.2_PUBLIC Directory, which is present inside Downloads, and we have run a command "./ghidraRun" to launch Ghidra so that we can proceed with our analysis of Wannacry.exe

Ghidra opens, then go to file > non-shared project > fill project name > Finish.

Select your project, then go to File> import file > navigate to WannaCry.exe > Ok > Ok > Open in Code Browser > Click yes for performing analysis > Analyze.

As shown in Fig. 6.1.1.4 here, you can analyze Wannacry.exe to detect malicious code, functions, etc.

```
  Decompile: entry - (Wannacry.exe)
 1
 2 /* WARNING: Globals starting with '_' overlap smaller symbols at the same address */
 3
 4 void entry(void)
 5
 6 {
 7    undefined4 *puVar1;
 8    uint uVar2;
 9    HMODULE pHVar3;
10    byte *pbVar4;
11    undefined4 uVar5;
12    char **local_74;
13    _startupinfo local_70;
14    int local_6c;
15    char **local_68;
16    int local_64;
17    _STARTUPINFOA local_60;
18    undefined1 *local_1c;
19    void *pvStack_14;
20    undefined *puStack_10;
21    undefined *puStack_c;
22    undefined4 local_8;
23
24    puStack_c = &DAT_0040d488;
25    puStack_10 = &DAT_004076f4;
26    pvStack_14 = ExceptionList;
27    local_1c = &stackOxffffff78;
28    local_8 = 0;
29    ExceptionList = &pvStack_14;
30    __set_app_type(2);
31    _DAT_0040f94c = 0xffffffff;
32    _DAT_0040f950 = 0xffffffff;
33    puVar1 = (undefined4 *)__p__fmode();
34    *puVar1 = DAT_0040f948;
35    puVar1 = (undefined4 *)__p__commode();
36    *puVar1 = DAT_0040f944;
37    _DAT_0040f954 = *(undefined4 *)_adjust_fdiv_exref;
38    FUN_0040793f();
39    if (DAT_0040f870 == 0) {
40      __setusermatherr(&LAB_0040793c);
41    }
42    FUN_0040792a();
43    initterm(&DAT_0040e008,&DAT_0040e00c);
44    local_70.newmode = DAT_0040f940;
45    __getmainargs(&local_64,&local_74,&local_68,_DoWildCard_0040f93c,&local_70);
46    initterm(&DAT_0040e000,&DAT_0040e004);
47    pbVar4 = *(byte **)_acmdln_exref;
48    if (*pbVar4 != 0x22) {
49      do {
```

Figure 6.1.1.4. This image tells us that we are analyzing WannaCry.exe using Ghidra decompiler, and the code is a blend of C and assembly language. This is the decompiled code of the entry point function, void entry(void), which represents the default entry point of the executable file. puStack_c and pvStack_14 represent static pointer initializations and static/global assignments. Fun_0040793f() and FUN_0040792a() are the function calls.

6.1.2 Cutter

Cutter is a an open-source reverse engineering platform powered by Rizin, and is available for free. It is designed to be progressive and an accommodated reverse engineering platform, keeping the user experience in mind. Cutter was developed by reverse engineers for reverse engineers.

This tool decompiles the object code into High-Level Language code (like C).

Steps to be followed to use Cutter:

- Open Terminal
- Navigate to Downloads, using the command in Fig. 6.1.2.1

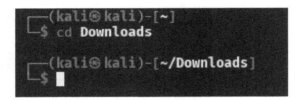

Figure 6.1.2.1 This is a terminal window in Kali Linux. The kali written in blue indicates the username as well as the hostname with a special character(~) informing us about the current directory in which we are operating. In the above figure, the command run is "cd Downloads," which takes us to the Downloads Directory, which is usually present inside the home directory.

- Open the cutter by giving the path to your Wannacry.exe, using the command in Fig. 6.1.2.2

```
┌──(kali㉿kali)-[~/Downloads]
└─$ cutter /home/kali/Downloads/Wannacry.exe
"0.7.4" "0.7.4"
```

Figure 6.1.2.2 This is a terminal window of Kali Linux, which tells us that we are inside the Downloads folder and there is an app image of the Cutter tool inside the Downloads folder. We are launching the cutter by giving the path of our WannaCry.exe by running the command "cutter /home/kali/Downloads/Wannacry.exe"

Open the file, select the file path, then click Open > Ok.

As shown in Fig. 6.1.2.3, You're now ready for analyzing your Wannacry.exe file for malicious content, function calls, etc.

```
entry0();
; var int32_t var_100h @ stack - 0x100
; var int32_t var_fch @ stack - 0xfc
; var int32_t var_f8h @ stack - 0xf8
; var int32_t var_f4h @ stack - 0xf4
; var int var_f0h @ stack - 0xf0
; var int32_t var_ech @ stack - 0xec
; var int32_t var_e8h @ stack - 0xe8
; var LPSTARTUPINFOA lpStartupInfo @ stack - 0xe4
; var int32_t var_b8h @ stack - 0xb8
; var int32_t var_b4h @ stack - 0xb4
; var int32_t var_9ch @ stack - 0x9c
; var int32_t var_8ch @ stack - 0x8c
; var int32_t var_88h @ stack - 0x88
; var int32_t var_1ch @ stack - 0x1c
; var int32_t var_14h @ stack - 0x14
0x004077ba      push    ebp
0x004077bb      mov     ebp, esp
0x004077bd      push    0xffffffffffffffff
0x004077bf      push    data.0040d488 ; 0x40d488
0x004077c4      push    data.004076f4 ; 0x4076f4
0x004077c9      mov     eax, dword fs:[0]
0x004077cf      push    eax
0x004077d0      mov     dword fs:[0], esp
0x004077d7      sub     esp, 0x68
0x004077da      push    ebx
0x004077db      push    esi
0x004077dc      push    edi
0x004077dd      mov     dword [var_1ch], esp
0x004077e0      xor     ebx, ebx
0x004077e2      mov     dword [var_8ch], ebx
0x004077e5      push    2          ; 2
0x004077e7      call    dword [__set_app_type] ; 0x4081c4
0x004077ed      pop     ecx
0x004077ee      or      dword [data.0040f94c], 0xffffffff ; 0x40f94c
0x004077f5      or      dword [data.0040f950], 0xffffffff ; 0x40f950
0x004077fc      call    dword [__p__fmode] ; 0x4081c0
0x00407802      mov     ecx, dword [data.0040f948] ; 0x40f948
0x00407808      mov     dword [eax], ecx
0x0040780a      call    dword [__p__commode] ; 0x4081bc
0x00407810      mov     ecx, dword [data.0040f944] ; 0x40f944
0x00407816      mov     dword [eax], ecx
0x00407818      mov     eax, dword [_adjust_fdiv] ; 0x4081b8
0x0040781d      mov     eax, dword [eax]
```

*Figure 6.1.2.3 This image shows us the assembly view of the entry()
function, when we have launched cutter tool for our analysis of
Wannacry.exe file. Cutter used disassembler for this purpose. As we can
see, multiple stack variables are declared using offsets like stack – 0x100,
which indicates frame setup of stack.*

6.1.3 Radare2

A libre/free tool for smoothing multiple low-level tasks like reverse engineering, forensics, debugging, binary analysis, exploiting, etc. It is made up of many libraries which are expanded with programs and plugins that can be made to operate on it's own with almost any programming language.

This tool converts the binary code into assembly instructions.

Steps to be followed to use radare2:

* Open Terminal
* Install Kali, using the command in Fig. 6.1.3.1

```
┌──(kali㉿kali)-[~/Downloads]
└─$ sudo apt install radare2
[sudo] password for kali:
```

Figure 6.1.3.1 This is a terminal window in the Kali Linux. The kali written in blue indicates the username as well as the hostname with a special character(~) informing us about the current directory in which we are operating. In the above Fig. the command run is "sudo apt install radare2" for installing radare2 on our Linux OS and asks for password to proceed with installation.

* Run radare2, using the command in Fig. 6.1.3.2

```
┌──(kali㉿kali)-[~]
└─$ r2 -A /home/kali/Downloads/Wannacry.exe
WARN: Relocs has not been applied. Please use `-e bin.relocs.
INFO: Analyze all flags starting with sym. and entry0 (aa)
INFO: Analyze imports (af@@@i)
```

Figure 6.1.3.2 This is a terminal window in the Kali Linux. The kali written in blue indicates the username as well as the hostname with a special character(~) informing us about the current directory in which we are operating. The command "-A" automatically analyses the Wannacry.exe binary file. Performs initial analysis with detection of symbols and begins importing function analysis.

Then, use "afl" for analysis of the Wannacry.exe file, as shown in Fig. 6.1.3.3

Figure 6.1.3.3 This image shows us the view when -afl command is run in radare2, listing all the functions discovered in the Wannacry.exe binary after performing analysis. 0x004077ba and so on represents address in hexa-decimal format, with different sizes and name.

6.1.4 Ret-Dec

It is a retargetable machine-code decompiler developed by Avast which is rooted on LLVM. This decompiler is not restricted to any specific target architecture, executable file format or operating system. It can be used for static analysis of executable files with detailed information. It can turn binaries (.exe files) into readable C code, which is helpful for our malware analysis.

This tool converts the machine code into High-Level Language code (like C or a similar HLL language).

Steps to be followed to use ret-dec:

- Open terminal
- Navigate to ret-dec, using the command in Fig. 6.1.4.1

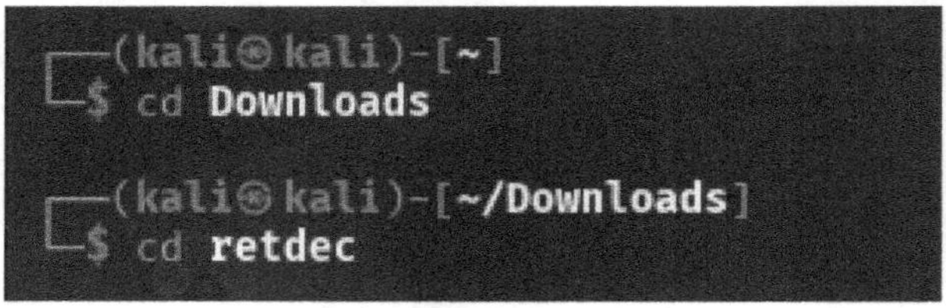

Figure 6.1.4.1 This is a terminal window in the Kali Linux. The kali written in blue indicates the username as well as the hostname with a special character(~) informing us about the current directory in which we are operating. In the above Fig. the command run is "cd Downloads" which takes us to the Downloads Directory, which is usually present inside the

home directory. Then, we navigate inside ret-dec folder which is inside Downloads.

- Now, decompile using the command in Fig. 6.1.4.2

```
┌──(kali㉿kali)-[~/Downloads/retdec/build]
└─$ retdec-decompiler /home/kali/Downloads/Wannacry.exe
```

Figure 6.1.4.2 This is a terminal window in the Kali Linux. The kali written in blue indicates the username as well as the hostname with a special character(~) informing us about the current directory in which we are operating, in the above figure we are inside the build folder and we are running the ret-dec decompiler to analyze Wannacry.exe by giving its path.

Wannacry.c file is saved in the same directory, as we can see in the Fig. 6.1.4.3

```
                                    kali@kali: ~/Downloads/retdec/build                                   
File  Actions  Edit  View  Help
// Address range: 0×4064bb - 0×4064e2
int32_t function_4064bb(int32_t a1, int32_t a2, int32_t a3, int32_t a4, int32_t a5, int32_t a6, int32_t a7, int32_t a8) {
    // 0×4064bb
    return function_4061e0(a1, a2, 0, a3, a4, a5, a6, a7, a8);
}

// Address range: 0×4064e2 - 0×406520
int32_t function_4064e2(int32_t a1) {
    int32_t result = -102; // 0×4064ec
    if (a1 ≠ 0) {
        // 0×4064f3
        *(int32_t *)(a1 + 20) = *(int32_t *)(a1 + 36);
        *(int32_t *)(a1 + 16) = 0;
        result = function_4061e0(a1, a1 + 40, a1 + 120, 0, 0, 0, 0, 0, 0);
        *(int32_t *)(a1 + 24) = (int32_t)(result == 0);
    }
    // 0×40651d
    return result;
}

// Address range: 0×406520 - 0×40657a
int32_t function_406520(int32_t a1) {
    // 0×406520
    if (a1 == 0) {
        // 0×406577
        return -102;
    }
    int32_t * v1 = (int32_t *)(a1 + 24); // 0×406530
    if (*v1 == 0) {
        // 0×406577
        return -100;
    }
    int32_t * v2 = (int32_t *)(a1 + 16); // 0×406535
    int32_t v3 = *v2 + 1; // 0×406538
    int32_t result = -100; // 0×40653c
    if (v3 ≠ *(int32_t *)(a1 + 4)) {
        int32_t v4 = *(int32_t *)(a1 + 76); // 0×406549
        *v2 = v3;
        int32_t * v5 = (int32_t *)(a1 + 20); // 0×406560
        *v5 = *(int32_t *)(a1 + 80) + 46 + *(int32_t *)(a1 + 72) + v4 + *v5;
        result = function_4061e0(a1, a1 + 40, a1 + 120, 0, 0, 0, 0, 0, 0);
        *v1 = (int32_t)(result == 0);
    }
    // 0×406577
    return result;
}
```

Figure 6.1.4.3 This image shows us the view when ret-dec decompiler is launched, decompiling Wannacry.exe for analysis. RetDec has decompiled the binary file in to High-Level Language C, and what we are seeing is C-like pseudocode, containing low-

level logic with integer manipulation, memory access patterns and calling functions using pointers.

6.1.5 Binary Ninja

Binary Ninja is a disassembler, interactive decompiler, integrated debugger, and a platform for binary analysis that serves as a reverse engineering platform developed by Vector 35 Inc. Using this, we can disassemble and visualize a binary file in both graph-based and linear views. The Debugger is written in C++ and is shipped with BN as a plugin. It is the most advanced platform for binary analysis and has a stack of unique related intermediate languages. High-Level IL is the default view, we can see it and observe that it almost reads like pseudocode.

This tool decompiles the object code into High-Level Language code (like C or C++) and also disassembles the code in to assembly instructions.

Steps to be followed to use Binary Ninja:

- Open the terminal
- Navigate to the Binary Ninja directory, using the command in Fig. 6.1.5.1

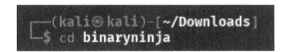

Figure 6.1.5.1 This is a terminal window in the Kali Linux. The kali written in blue indicates the username as well as the hostname with a special character(~) informing us about the current directory in which we are operating. In the above Fig., we are inside the Downloads Directory, and we want to navigate inside binary ninja using the command "cd binaryninja".

- Launch Binary Ninja, using the command in Fig. 6.1.5.2

Figure 6.1.5.2 This image tells us that we are using Kali Linux terminal, and we are inside our binaryninja Directory which is present inside Downloads then, run the command "./binaryninja" to launch it so, that we can proceed with our analysis of Wannacry.exe

Now, our Wannacry.exe is ready for analysis as shown in Fig. 6.1.5.3

Figure 6.1.5.3 This image shows us the view when binaryninja is launched, to analyze Wannacry.exe. The image contains a section of DOS Header(struct DOS_Header __dos_header) and Rich Header(struct Rich_Header __rich_header). e_magic= "MZ", MZ stands for Mark Zbikowski who was a Microsoft architect. This is a signature which indicates that this is a DOS-compatible and executable.

6.1.6 *Obj-dump*

Obj-dump is a lightweight and powerful tool for inspecting and disassembling binaries which forms a perfect basis for basic static analysis, and it is built with Kali Linux. It comes installed as a part of the package named "binutils".

This tool can be used as a disassembler, to view your executable file in assembly language.

Steps to follow to use obj-dump:

- Open Terminal

- Use obj-dump for analysis of our Wannacry.exe file, using the command in Fig. 6.1.6.1

```
┌──(kali㉿kali)-[~/Downloads]
└─$ objdump -s /home/kali/Downloads/Wannacry.exe

/home/kali/Downloads/Wannacry.exe:     file format pei-i386
```

Figure 6.1.6.1 This image tells us that we are using the Kali Linux terminal, and we are inside our Downloads Directory and we have run a command "objdump -s /home/kali/Downloads/Wannacry.exe" to launch it so, that we can proceed with our analysis of Wannacry.exe. -s stands for full contents of all sections. pei-i386 means that the given file is PE(Portable Executable) for intel architecture(x86) of 32 bit.

The analysis is as shown in Fig. 6.1.6.2

```
Contents of section .text:
 401000 5633f639 74240c57 7407681c e04000eb   V3.9t$.Wt.h..@..
 401010 056818e0 40006810 e04000ff 15188140   .h..@.h..@.....@
 401020 008bf859 3bfe5975 0433c0eb 34397424   ...Y;.Yu.3..49t$
 401030 10576a01 680c0300 00ff7424 187408ff   .Wj.h.....t$.t..
 401040 15148140 00eb06ff 15108140 0083c410   ...@......@....
 401050 85c07403 6a015e57 ff150c81 4000598b   ..t.j.^W....@.Y.
 401060 c65f5ec3 558bec83 ec545657 6a1033c0   ._^.U....TVWj.3.
 401070 598d7db0 c745ac44 00000033 f6f3ab8d   Y.}..E.D...3....
 401080 7df48975 f0ababab 6a018d45 f05f6689   }..u....j..E._f.
 401090 75dc508d 45ac5056 56680000 00085656   u.P.E.PVVh....VV
 4010a0 56897dd8 ff750856 ff15ec80 400085c0   V.}..u.V....@...
 4010b0 74453975 0c742cff 750cff75 f0ff15f4   tE9u.t,.u..u....
 4010c0 80400085 c0740b6a ffff75f0 ff15f880   .@...t.j..u.....
 4010d0 40003975 10740cff 7510ff75 f0ff15fc   @.9u.t..u..u....
 4010e0 804000ff 75f08b35 f0804000 ffd6ff75   .@..u..5..@....u
 4010f0 f4ffd68b c7eb0233 c05f5ec9 c3558bec   .......3._^..U.
 401100 81ecdc02 00005657 6a05be4c e0400059   ......VWj..L.@.Y
 401110 8dbd2cff fffff3a5 6a2d33c0 208524fd   ..,....j-3. .$.
 401120 ffff598d bd40ffff ff8365fc 00f3abb9   ..Y..@....e.....
 401130 81000000 8dbd25fd fffff3ab 66abaa8d   ......%.....f..
 401140 852cffff ff6834e0 400050ff 15348140   .,....h4.@.P..4.@
 401150 008365f8 005959bf 30e04000 8d45fc33   ..e..YY.0.@..E.3
 401160 f63975f8 508d852c ffffff50 75076802   .9u.P..,...Pu.h.
 401170 000080eb 05680100 0080ff15 14804000   .....h........@.
 401180 3975fc0f 84840000 00397508 743e8d85   9u.......9u.t>..
 401190 24fdffff 50680702 0000ff15 d4804000   $...Ph........@.
 4011a0 8d8524fd ffff50e8 08650000 5940508d   ..$...P..e...Y@P.
 4011b0 8524fdff ff506a01 5657ff75 fcff1518   .$...Pj.VW.u....
 4011c0 8040008b f0f7de1b f646eb34 8d45f4c7   .@.......F.4.E..
 4011d0 45f40702 0000508d 8524fdff ff505656   E.....P..$...PVV
 4011e0 57ff75fc ff151c80 40008bf0 f7de1bf6   W.u.....@.......
```

Figure 6.1.6.2 This image shows us the view when obj-dump is launched, to analyze Wannacry.exe. we can see hex+ASCII dump of the .text section of our binary Wannacry.exe, which was produced by the command in fig. 8.4.6.2. ".text section" is the code section in a PE file which contains the machine executable instructions that is the core logic of a program.

6.2 DYNAMIC ANALYSIS

In this, let's run and execute the Wannacry.exe on our Windows OS in a virtual environment.

- First of all, open Windows Defender and then turn off Real-Time protection and Ransomware protection then proceed further else, Wannacry.exe could be blocked.
- After, downloading WannaCry from Wannacry.exe
- Double click > yes
- A pop-up as below is displayed, Click Run as shown in Figure 6.2.1

Figure 6.2.1 As we can see clearly, this is a security warning dialog in the Windows Operating System that asks us the permission to run Wannacry.exe or not. This also tells us about the name of the file that we are about to run and its path as well that is, "C:\Users\Manikya\Downloads\Wannacry.exe" whose publisher is unknown, and the warning message is written in bold "The publisher could not be verified. Are you sure you want to run this software?" And, in the last, we can see a hyperlink-"How can I decide what software to run?"

- Your Downloads folder which had only Wannacry.exe previously, could be like this after running the ransomware, as shown in Figure 6.2.2

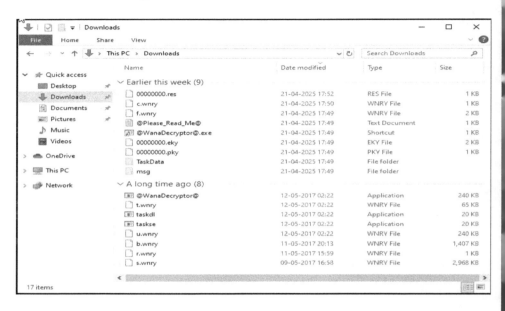

Figure 6.2.2 As we can see clearly, that this is the Downloads folder in File Explorer, which contains files that are associated with WannaCry after, it was run. The file explorer has divided the files in two major parts, A long time ago and earlier this week containing 8 and 9 files respectively with their timestamps which tells us when they were downloaded, edited or created most recently.

- Your window looks like this before launching WannaCry ransomware as shown in Figure 6.2.3

Figure 6.2.3 This image tells us that Windows is setup in virtual machine created inside Oracle VirtualBox, with two icons on the desktop that is, Recycle Bin and Microsoft Edge Browser. We can also tell that this is Windows 10, with five default icons on the taskbar, and to the extreme right corner of the windows is Date and Time with 2 recent notifications. This image represents the state of the windows before running WannaCry.

- Now, your windows look like this as shown in Figure 6.2.4

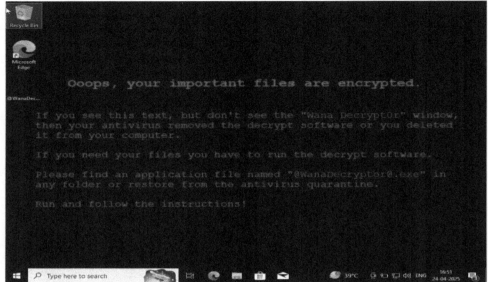

Figure 6.2.4 **This image tells us that Windows has three icons on the desktop that is, Recycle Bin, Microsoft Edge Browser, and WannaCry Decryptor. We can also tell that this is Windows 10, with five default icons on the taskbar, and to the extreme right corner of the window is Date and Time with 3 recent notifications. This image represents the state of the windows after running WannaCry. The default wallpaper of Windows is changed and currently reads a message "Ooops, your important files are encrypted".**

- Ransomware is defined as a malicious software which encrypts the personal data of a victim until a ransom that is, a monetary amount is paid in the form of difficult-to-trace payment details such as cryptocurrencies, like Bitcoin and other cryptocurrencies.

- The image mentioned below asks for the same, as shown in Figure 6.2.5

```
@Please_Read_Me@ - Notepad                                                                    —   □   ×
File  Edit  Format  View  Help
Q:  What's wrong with my files?

A:  Ooops, your important files are encrypted. It means you will not be able to access them anymore until they are decrypted.
    If you follow our instructions, we guarantee that you can decrypt all your files quickly and safely!
    Let's start decrypting!

Q:  What do I do?

A:  First, you need to pay service fees for the decryption.
    Please send $300 worth of bitcoin to this bitcoin address: 13AM4VW2dhxYgXeQepoHkHSQuy6NgaEb94

    Next, please find an application file named "@WanaDecryptor@.exe". It is the decrypt software.
    Run and follow the instructions! (You may need to disable your antivirus for a while.)

Q:  How can I trust?

A:  Don't worry about decryption.
    We will decrypt your files surely because nobody will trust us if we cheat users.

*   If you need our assistance, send a message by clicking <Contact Us> on the decryptor window.
```

*Figure **6.2.5** This image tells us that there is a text file named "@Please_Read_Me@" and is currently opened in Notepad. This text file contains 3 questions represented by "Q" followed by their respective answers represented by "A". These questions inform the user about what has happened to their system and how they can regain control of their system. This file was created after WannaCry was run.*

Figure 6.2.6 This image tells us that Windows has four icons on the desktop that is, Recycle Bin, Microsoft Edge Browser, and WannaCry Decryptors. We can also tell that this is Windows 10, with five default icons on the taskbar, and to the extreme right corner of the windows is Date and Time with 1 recent notification. This image represents the state of the windows after running WannaCry as we can tell this after reading the open dialog box displayed on the windows in red color. It tells the user to make a ransom payment to re-access their files otherwise, files can be lost on 28/4/2025, 17:50, and also runs a timer for days left.

Chapter 7

Result and Discussion

7.1 Analysis of malicious code

Let's look at the malicious code present inside the Wannacry.exe that is provided to us by the reverse engineering tools like Ghidra, Cutter, Radare2, Binary Ninja, Ret-Dec, and Obj Dump.

7.1.1   Ghidra

```
 Decompile: entry - (Wannacry.exe)
 1
 2 /* WARNING: Globals starting with '_' overlap smaller symbols at the same address */
 3
 4 void entry(void)
 5
 6 {
 7   undefined4 *puVar1;
 8   uint uVar2;
 9   HMODULE pHVar3;
10   byte *pbVar4;
11   undefined4 uVar5;
12   char **local_74;
13   _startupinfo local_70;
14   int local_6c;
15   char **local_68;
16   int local_64;
17   _STARTUPINFOA local_60;
18   undefined1 *local_1c;
19   void *pvStack_14;
20   undefined *puStack_10;
21   undefined *puStack_c;
22   undefined4 local_8;
23
24   puStack_c = &DAT_0040d488;
25   puStack_10 = &DAT_004076f4;
26   pvStack_14 = ExceptionList;
27   local_1c = &stackOxffffff78;
28   local_8 = 0;
29   ExceptionList = &pvStack_14;
30   __set_app_type(2);
31   _DAT_0040f94c = 0xffffffff;
32   _DAT_0040f950 = 0xffffffff;
33   puVar1 = (undefined4 *)__p__fmode();
34   *puVar1 = DAT_0040f948;
35   puVar1 = (undefined4 *)__p__commode();
36   *puVar1 = DAT_0040f944;
37   _DAT_0040f954 = *(undefined4 *)_adjust_fdiv_exref;
38   FUN_0040793f();
39   if (DAT_0040f870 == 0) {
40     __setusermatherr(&LAB_0040793c);
41   }
42   FUN_0040792a();
43   initterm(&DAT_0040e008,&DAT_0040e00c);
44   local_70.newmode = DAT_0040f940;
45   __getmainargs(&local_64,&local_74,&local_68,_DoWildCard_0040f93c,&local_70);
46   initterm(&DAT_0040e000,&DAT_0040e004);
47   pbVar4 = *(byte **)_acmdln_exref;
48   if (*pbVar4 != 0x22) {
49     do {
```

Figure 7.1.1 This image tells us that we are analyzing WannaCry.exe using Ghidra decompiler, and the code is a blend of C and assembly language. This is the decompiled code of the entry point function, void entry(void), which represents the default entry point of the executable file. puStack_c and pvStack_14 represent static pointer initializations and static/global assignments. Fun_0040793f() and FUN_0040792a() are the function calls.

Analysis of the above code is as below:

- The function, entry(void) prepares the runtime environment before executing the main payload, typically present in Windows program but, given the context this function may serve as a starting point for unwanted activity.

- exit(local_6c)
  - exits with return code from FUN_00401fe7(..), without result checking
  - acts as a wrapper for malicious code

- FUN_0040793f();
  FUN_0040792a();
  local_6c = FUN_00401fe7(pHVar3,uVar5,pbVar4,uVar2);
  The above functions are not standard APIs and maybe a part of the ransomware logic.
  - FUN_00401fe7(…) is most suspicious as it receives:
    - module handle (GetModuleHandleA(0)),

- o uVar5 (zero),
- o Parsed command-line pointer (pbVar4),
- o Drops the ransomware payload
- o Launches encryption routines
- o Spreading mechanisms (SMB exploit)

7.1.2 Cutter

```
entry0();
; var int32_t var_100h @ stack - 0x100
; var int32_t var_fch @ stack - 0xfc
; var int32_t var_f8h @ stack - 0xf8
; var int32_t var_f4h @ stack - 0xf4
; var int var_f0h @ stack - 0xf0
; var int32_t var_ech @ stack - 0xec
; var int32_t var_e8h @ stack - 0xe8
; var LPSTARTUPINFOA lpStartupInfo @ stack - 0xe4
; var int32_t var_b8h @ stack - 0xb8
; var int32_t var_b4h @ stack - 0xb4
; var int32_t var_9ch @ stack - 0x9c
; var int32_t var_8ch @ stack - 0x8c
; var int32_t var_88h @ stack - 0x88
; var int32_t var_1ch @ stack - 0x1c
; var int32_t var_14h @ stack - 0x14
0x004077ba      push    ebp
0x004077bb      mov     ebp, esp
0x004077bd      push    0xffffffffffffffff
0x004077bf      push    data.0040d488 ; 0x40d488
0x004077c4      push    data.004076f4 ; 0x4076f4
0x004077c9      mov     eax, dword fs:[0]
0x004077cf      push    eax
0x004077d0      mov     dword fs:[0], esp
0x004077d7      sub     esp, 0x68
0x004077da      push    ebx
0x004077db      push    esi
0x004077dc      push    edi
0x004077dd      mov     dword [var_1ch], esp
0x004077e0      xor     ebx, ebx
0x004077e2      mov     dword [var_8ch], ebx
0x004077e5      push    2           ; 2
0x004077e7      call    dword [__set_app_type] ; 0x4081c4
0x004077ed      pop     ecx
0x004077ee      or      dword [data.0040f94c], 0xffffffff ; 0x40f94c
0x004077f5      or      dword [data.0040f950], 0xffffffff ; 0x40f950
0x004077fc      call    dword [__p__fmode] ; 0x4081c0
0x00407802      mov     ecx, dword [data.0040f948] ; 0x40f948
0x00407808      mov     dword [eax], ecx
0x0040780a      call    dword [__p__commode] ; 0x4081bc
0x00407810      mov     ecx, dword [data.0040f944] ; 0x40f944
0x00407816      mov     dword [eax], ecx
0x00407818      mov     eax, dword [_adjust_fdiv] ; 0x4081b8
0x0040781d      mov     eax, dword [eax]
```

*Figure 7.1.2 This image shows us the assembly view of the entry()
function, when we have launched cutter tool for our analysis of
Wannacry.exe file. Cutter used disassembler for this purpose. As we can
see, multiple stack variables are declared using offsets like stack – 0x100,
which indicates frame setup of stack.*

Analysis of the above code is as below:

- esi = *(imp._acmdln); // get command line

  ...

  if (*(esi) != 0x22) { ... }

  This section parses the command-line string manually, neglecting
  higher-level API parsing. It is generally observed in malware
  droppers, extracting arguments or embedding payloads.

- eax = GetModuleHandleA (...);

  eax = main ();

  exit (eax);

  - The call to main() is actually a malicious payload – this
    function is not named here but might be same as
    FUN_00401fe7(...) from 7.1.1.
  - There is no wmain or WinMain; it directly invokes a
    suspicious payload after little setup.
- eax = *(var_9ch);

  ecx = *(eax);

  ecx = *(ecx);

_XcptFilter (ecx, eax);

- o After calling exit(), running exception filtering is highly unusual.
- o Might be a trick to complicate or a leftover from error handling.
- o Hiding payload crashes from being logged or visible.

7.1.3 Radare2

Figure 7.1.3 This image shows us the view when -afl command is run in radare2, listing all the functions discovered in the Wannacry.exe binary after performing analysis. 0x004077ba and so on represents address in hexa-decimal format, with different sizes and name.

Analysis of the above code is as below:

Unusually Large Functions containing obfuscated or complex logic:

- 0x00403cfc (1419 bytes) – likely contains core malicious conduct such as encryption routines or payload execution; very large function.
- 0x00406c40 (1072 bytes) – possibly related to SMB exploit logic or network propagation; also, very large.
- 0x00402a76 (1032 bytes) – Could involve file enumeration logic or core encryption (AES).

Targets for further analysis:

- 0x00403cfc: likely the heart of ransomware logic (file operations or encryption).
- 0x00406c40: Higher chance that it contains propagation logic.
- 0x00402a76 and 0x0040514d: Could be decryption of embedded data, unpacking or payload control.

7.1.4 Ret-Dec

```
// Address range: 0×4064bb - 0×4064e2
int32_t function_4064bb(int32_t a1, int32_t a2, int32_t a3, int32_t a4, int32_t a5, int32_t a6, int32_t a7, int32_t a8) {
    // 0×4064bb
    return function_4061e0(a1, a2, 0, a3, a4, a5, a6, a7, a8);
}

// Address range: 0×4064e2 - 0×406520
int32_t function_4064e2(int32_t a1) {
    int32_t result = -102; // 0×4064ec
    if (a1 ≠ 0) {
        // 0×4064f3
        *(int32_t *)(a1 + 20) = *(int32_t *)(a1 + 36);
        *(int32_t *)(a1 + 16) = 0;
        result = function_4061e0(a1, a1 + 40, a1 + 120, 0, 0, 0, 0, 0, 0);
        *(int32_t *)(a1 + 24) = (int32_t)(result == 0);
    }
    // 0×40651d
    return result;
}

// Address range: 0×406520 - 0×40657a
int32_t function_406520(int32_t a1) {
    // 0×406520
    if (a1 == 0) {
        // 0×406577
        return -102;
    }
    int32_t * v1 = (int32_t *)(a1 + 24); // 0×406530
    if (*v1 == 0) {
        // 0×406577
        return -100;
    }
    int32_t * v2 = (int32_t *)(a1 + 16); // 0×406535
    int32_t v3 = *v2 + 1; // 0×406538
    int32_t result = -100; // 0×40653c
    if (v3 ≠ *(int32_t *)(a1 + 4)) {
        int32_t v4 = *(int32_t *)(a1 + 76); // 0×406549
        *v2 = v3;
        int32_t * v5 = (int32_t *)(a1 + 20); // 0×406560
        *v5 = *(int32_t *)(a1 + 80) + 46 + *(int32_t *)(a1 + 72) + v4 + *v5;
        result = function_4061e0(a1, a1 + 40, a1 + 120, 0, 0, 0, 0, 0, 0);
        *v1 = (int32_t)(result == 0);
    }
    // 0×406577
    return result;
}
```

Figure 7.1.4 This image shows us the view when ret-dec decompiler is launched, decompiling Wannacry.exe for analysis. RetDec has decompiled the binary file in to High-Level Language C, and what we are seeing is C-like pseudocode, containing low-level logic with integer manipulation, memory access patterns and calling functions using pointers.

Analysis of the above code is as below:

- function_4064e2(int32_t a1)

  if (a1 == 0) return -102;

  *(int32_t *)(a1 + 20) = *(int32_t *)(a1 + 36);

  *(int32_t *)(a1 + 16) = 0;

  result = function_4061e0(a1, a1 + 40, a1 + 120, 0, 0, 0, 0, 0);

  *(int32_t *)(a1 + 24) = (int32_t)(result == 0);

  return result;

  - Pointer manipulation is happening, particularly reading/writing from offsets.
  - function_4061e0() is called with various offsets from a1, and the result calculates the value at a1 + 24.

  Why Suspicious?

  - function might be modifying or initializing a structure in memory.
  - Use of raw memory offsets suggests either encryption/decryption routines or custom data structures.

- function_406520(int32_t a1)
  - This function depends on previous values (a1 + 16, a1 + 24, etc.).
  - function_4061e0() is called again.

o v5 is calculated using multiple offset additions and ,
possibly building a pointer or buffer.

Why suspicious?

o Repeated calls to function_4061e0 with consistent
parameters actually points to an encryption, I/O or
hashing operation.

o The use of hardcoded multipliers (* 46, + 72, etc.) and
offsets is typical in obfuscated code to avoid detection.

Taking the context of WannaCry, and based on the above signs:

- Heavy use of memory offsetting and pointer arithmetic
- Function calls operating on several memory regions
- State flags being set to (*(a1 + 24) = result == 0)

These functions are actually part of WannaCry's internal logic for key
management or encryption.

7.1.5 Obj Dump

```
Contents of section .text:
 401000 5633f639 74240c57 7407681c e04000eb  V3.9t$.Wt.h..@..
 401010 056818e0 40006810 e04000ff 15188140  .h..@.h..@.....@
 401020 008bf859 3bfe5975 0433c0eb 34397424  ...Y;.Yu.3..49t$
 401030 10576a01 680c0300 00ff7424 187408ff  .Wj.h.....t$.t..
 401040 15148140 00eb06ff 15108140 0083c410  ...@.....@....
 401050 85c07403 6a015e57 ff150c81 4000598b  ..t.j.^W...@.Y.
 401060 c65f5ec3 558bec83 ec545657 6a1033c0  ._^.U....TVWj.3.
 401070 598d7db0 c745ac44 00000033 f6f3ab8d  Y.}..E.D...3...
 401080 7df48975 f0ababab 6a018d45 f05f6689  }..u....j..E._f.
 401090 75dc508d 45ac5056 56680000 00085656  u.P.E.PVVh....VV
 4010a0 56897dd8 ff750856 ff15ec80 400085c0  V.}..u.V...@...
 4010b0 74453975 0c742cff 750cff75 f0ff15f4  tE9u.t,.u..u....
 4010c0 80400085 c0740b6a ffff75f0 ff15f880  .@...t.j..u.....
 4010d0 40003975 10740cff 7510ff75 f0ff15fc  @.9u.t..u..u....
 4010e0 804000ff 75f08b35 f0804000 ffd6ff75  .@..u..5..@....u
 4010f0 f4ffd68b c7eb0233 c05f5ec9 c3558bec  .......3._^..U.
 401100 81ecdc02 00005657 6a05be4c e0400059  ......VWj..L.@.Y
 401110 8dbd2cff fffff3a5 6a2d33c0 208524fd  ..,....j-3. .$.
 401120 ffff598d bd40ffff ff8365fc 00f3abb9  ..Y..@.....e....
 401130 81000000 8dbd25fd fffff3ab 66abaa8d  ......%.....f...
 401140 852cffff ff6834e0 400050ff 15348140  .,...h4.@.P..4.@
 401150 008365f8 005959bf 30e04000 8d45fc33  ..e..YY.0..@..E.3
 401160 f63975f8 508d852c ffffff50 75076802  .9u.P..,...Pu.h.
 401170 000080eb 05680100 0080ff15 14804000  .....h......@.
 401180 3975fc0f 84840000 00397508 743e8d85  9u......9u.t>..
 401190 24fdffff 50680702 0000ff15 d4804000  $...Ph......@.
 4011a0 8d8524fd ffff50e8 08650000 5940508d  ..$...P..e..Y@P.
 4011b0 8524fdff ff506a01 5657ff75 fcff1518  .$...Pj.VW.u....
 4011c0 8040008b f0f7de1b f646eb34 8d45f4c7  .@.......F.4.E..
 4011d0 45f40702 0000508d 8524fdff ff505656  E.....P..$...PVV
 4011e0 57ff75fc ff151c80 40008bf0 f7de1bf6  W.u.....@.......
```

Figure 7.1.5 This image shows us the view when obj-dump is launched, to analyze Wannacry.exe. we can see hex+ASCII dump of the .text section of our binary Wannacry.exe, which was produced by the command in fig. 8.4.6.2. ".text section" is the code section in a PE file which contains the machine executable instructions that is the core logic of a program.

Analysis of the above code is as below:

- Obfuscated Code

  Various locations (e.g., at addresses 0x401080, 0x401050, 0x401100, etc.) show sequences of 00, ff, eb, and e8, which are common in:

  - NOP sleds
  - Call instructions (e8)
  - Jump instructions (eb)
  - Used heavily in packed or obfuscated payloads
  - Look at: 401090: 598d7db0 c745ac44 000003d3 f6f38ad0

    c7 45 ac 44 00 00 03 → mov dword ptr [ebp-54h], 0x300044

    This could be memory preparation for malicious logic.

- Suspicious Use of e8 Calls (likely to shellcode loaders)

  Look at: 401000: 5633f639 74240c57 7407681c e04000eb

  - eb is typically used in shellcode, a short JMP.
  - e8 is a CALL instruction, followed by a relative offset.

These are the signs of obfuscated function dispatchers or shellcode loaders.

- Data XOR Patterns or Key Expansion (Ransomware Traits)

  Patterns like: 4010c0: f4ffd68b 7e0b2033 c05f5ec9 c3505e0c

  - Appear to contain xor, ret and mov instruction patterns, mostly used in encryption loops.
  - If f4ffd68b corresponds to mov edx, [eax-0Ch] or similar, it could be part of decryption/encryption logic.

7.2 COMPARATIVE ANALYSIS

Static Analysis

- This involves the analysis of malware code without implementing it, focusing on functions, and malicious code.
- In this, we used various tools available for reverse engineering such as Ghidra, Cutter, Radare2, Ret-Dec, Binary Ninja and obj-dump.
- One by one we launched each of the tools and run them according to the steps mentioned in 8.4.
- Using, these tools we can see the malicious code present inside the .exe file that encrypts our windows.
- It uses automated tools like disassemblers and de-compilers for the analysis of ransomware.

- It involves less risk as it only converts the code into different languages using disassemblers and de-compilers.

Dynamic Analysis

- This analysis involves running malware, in a virtual environment setup with Windows installed on Virtual Box to observe its real-time.

- In this, we have setup windows using ISO file and proceed with the steps as mentioned in 8.3 to setup our Windows OS.

- Now, download WannaCry ransomware, and then install it on our virtual environment.

- In this, we observe how the ransomware behaves and encrypts the windows.

- It uses a real-time virtual environment for analysis of ransomware.

- It involves more risk as we install the ransomware file on our Windows OS.

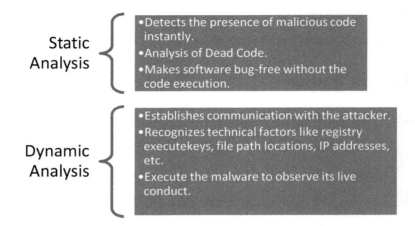

Static Analysis
- Detects the presence of malicious code instantly.
- Analysis of Dead Code.
- Makes software bug-free without the code execution.

Dynamic Analysis
- Establishes communication with the attacker.
- Recognizes technical factors like registry executekeys, file path locations, IP addresses, etc.
- Execute the malware to observe its live conduct.

Figure 7.2 As we can clearly see that this image tells us about the difference between Static and Dynamic analysis of malware, in this case WannaCry Ransomware. We can clearly see that the image is divided in two parts first, orange which tells us about the Static analysis and then green part which tells us about the Dynamic analysis containing four points each clearly explaining both types of analysis.

Chapter 8

Conclusion and Future Scope

CONCLUSION

Malware is a phrase that stands for "malicious software", which implies any type of software that harms various devices, steals or encrypts their data, and causes havoc. This should be referred to as a bug because both are different, as the bug is caused by accident, but malware is intentionally planted by the attackers to cause harm.

WannaCry ransomware's dynamic analysis provided insights that are useful into the malware itself, its encryption, and propagation mechanisms utilized by the ransomware, which caused havoc in organizations globally. Through controlled running in a sandbox or VirtualBox environment, the project was able to observe and document the ransomware's interaction with system resources, network communication, and its propagation through impacted hardware successfully. Utilizing equipment which is advanced, such as network analyzers, process monitors, and malware sandboxes, we were able to observe a real-time understanding of how WannaCry spreads across networks, encrypts the user's data, and takes advantage of the factors that make Windows vulnerable (like EternalBlue) to such attacks.

The result of the analysis tells us the importance of frequent patch management since WannaCry hit Windows PCs that were not patched.

In addition to that, studies of its Command and Control (C&C) communication and encryption also provided crucial information on how ransomware evolves and mutate to remain hidden. This information is of immense importance to help us improve existing cybersecurity models and devise more effective defense systems, such as intrusion prevention systems, patching policies, and ransomware-focused countermeasures.

Moreover, this project highlights various cybersecurity measures and advises regular software updates, network segmentation, and enhanced real-time monitoring to prevent such attacks in the future. As diverse ransomware types continue to emerge, insights from the analysis of the previous malware help researchers, cybersecurity professionals, and organizations to be better equipped to detect, counter, and recover from similar incidents. Every organization should focus on protecting its data by using the methods or tools provided by cybersecurity, analyzing any type of mishap, even from its internal employees, vendors, and anything that seems suspicious. If any suspicious activity is detected then the organization should respond quickly and better be prepared for similar types of malware attacks to prevent the loss of confidential information which can impact the organization as well as its employees in a negative way such as trades of the company, bank details of the organizations, personal information of the employees such as details related to bank accounts, social security number(SSN), family details and so on.

This project sheds light on the significance of both static and dynamic analysis, which helps us to understand complex cyber threats, providing details of the data that can be used to develop a safer and secure digital environment. By enhancing our understanding of WannaCry's behavior, we can learn to improve cybersecurity defenses, which limit the impact of ransomware and prevent the recurrence of such attacks throughout the world.

FUTURE SCOPE

The WannaCry ransomware's analysis has shed light on much of its behavior, encryption methods, and strategies on how it spread. However, there are various aspects where research and development can be explored further to enhance our understanding and defense against ransomware attacks in the future. This analysis will also help in mitigating risks associated and devising strategies to combat similar attacks in the upcoming timeline.

The future direction of this project is:

- Analysis of New Ransomware Variants: Because WannaCry is merely one of numerous ransomware strains, future research can look into analyzing new variants that could utilize the same or better methods. This will assist in discovering upcoming trends in ransomware attacks and developing preemptive defense measures.

- <u>Real-Time Detection System Development:</u> Based on the results of this analysis, the creation of sophisticated, real-time ransomware detection systems can be undertaken. Such systems would employ machine learning, behavioral detection, and anomaly detection to recognize ransomware operations in real time, minimizing response time and harm.

- <u>Automated Ransomware Analysis Frameworks:</u> Although manual dynamic analysis has been helpful, the malware analysis future is in automation. Creating automated frameworks to analyze ransomware within sandboxed environments, such as sophisticated sandboxing systems capable of mimicking compound networked environments, will speed the identification of new threats and enable quicker response.

- <u>Ransomware Decryption Tools:</u> Although certain ransomware variants have established decryption techniques, the fast pace of new method development tends to make them obsolete. Ongoing research into the creation of universal decryption tools and techniques for various ransomware types, such as using techniques like key recovery and reverse engineering, will be essential.

- <u>Research on Ransomware-as-a-Service (RaaS):</u> As ransomware becomes more commercially available through Ransomware-as-a-Service (RaaS) platforms, future research might be directed toward understanding how the platforms operate and how to target the infrastructure underpinning ransomware attacks. Knowing the dynamics of how RaaS operates might help in identifying attackers and breaking up cybercrime networks.

- <u>Cybersecurity Awareness and Education:</u> With ransomware evolving, awareness education among organizations and individuals regarding the threats, prevention, and recovery methods will be imperative.

Reverse engineering tools used are as follows with their logos:

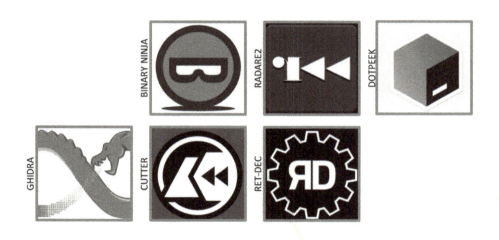

REFERENCES

1. R. A. Awad and K. D. Sayre, "Automatic Clustering of Malware Variants", *2016 IEEE Conference on Intelligence and Security Informatics (ISI 2016)*, pp. 298-303, 2016.

2. J. M. Ceron, C. B. Margi and L. Z. Granville, "MARS: An SDN-based Malware Analysis Solution", *2016 IEEE Symposium on Computers and Communication (ISCC)*, pp. 525-530, June 2016.

3. J. Friedman and M. Bouchard, Definitive Guide to Cyber Threat Intelligence: Using Knowledge about Adversaries to Win the War against Targeted Attacks, Cyberedge Press, pp. 1-60, 2015.

4. A. Fujino, J. Murakami and T. Mori, "Discovering Similar Malware Samples Using API Call Topics", *2015 12th Annual IEEE Consumer Communications and Networking Conference (CCNC)*, pp. 140-147, Jan 2015.

5. S. S. Hansen, T. M. T. Larsen, M. Stevanovic and J. M. Pedersen, "An Approach for Detection and Family Classification of Malware Based on Behavioral Analysis", *2016 International*

Conference on Computing Networking and Communications (ICNC), pp. 1-5, Feb 2016.

6. C. H. Malin, E. Casey, J. M. Aquilina and C. W. Rose, Malware Forensics Field Guide for Windows Systems: Digital Forensics Field, Elsevier Inc., pp. 363-400, 2012.

7. A. Kharaz, S. Arshad, C. Mulliner, W. Robertson and E. Kirda, "UNVEIL: A Large-Scale Automated Approach to Detecting Ransomware", *25th USENIX Security Symposium (USENIX Security 16)*, pp. 757-772, 2016.

8. Nokuthaba Siphambili, Oyena Mahlasela, Errol Baloyi, Elekanyani Mukondeleli, "A Review of the South African Public Sector's Capability in Combating Ransomware", 2024 4th International Multidisciplinary Information Technology and Engineering Conference (IMITEC), pp.493-499, 2024.

9. Meland PH, Bayoumy YFF, Sindre G. The ransomware-as-a-service economy within the darknet. *Comput Secur.* 2020; **92**:101762. doi:10.1016/j.cose.2020.101762

10. Al-rimy, B.A.S.; Maarof, M.A.; Shaid, S.Z.M. *A 0-Day Aware Crypto-Ransomware Early Behavioral Detection Framework*; Springer International Publishing: Cham, Germany, 2018.

www.ingramcontent.com/pod-product-compliance
Lightning Source LLC
LaVergne TN
LVHW041219050326
832903LV00021B/696